Herb Of Grace

ROSA NOUCHETTE CAREY

HERB OF GRACE

BY ROSA NOUCHETTE CAREY

12mo. Cloth, 75 cents per volume

Wooed and Married	Barbara Heathcote's Trial
Nellie's Memories	For Lilias
Queenie's Whim	Heriot's Choice
Not Like Other Girls	Wee Wifie
Mary St. John	Uncle Max
Robert Ord's Atonement	Only the Governess

The Search for Basil Lyndhurst

12mo. Cloth, $1.25 per volume

The Mistress of Brae Farm	Mollie's Prince
Other People's Lives	Rue with a Difference

Herb of Grace

In Lippincott's Series of Select Novels

12mo. Cloth, $1.00; paper, 50 cents

The Old, Old Story	Mrs. Romney
But Men Must Work	Sir Godfrey's Grand-daughters

BOOKS FOR GIRLS

Illustrated. 12mo. Cloth, gilt top, 75 cents per volume

Esther	Merle's Crusade
Aunt Diana	Our Bessie
Averil	

LIBRARY FOR GIRLS

Five volumes in box. $6.25. Also sold separately

Dr. Luttrell's First Patient	My Lady Frivol
Little Miss Muffet	Life's Trivial Round
Cousin Mona	